Sports for Supergirls

Combat Sports

Louise Spilsbury

Gareth Stevens
PUBLISHING

Please visit our website, **www.garethstevens.com**.
For a free color catalog of all our high-quality books,
call toll free 1-800-542-2595 or fax 1-877-542-2596.

Cataloging-in-Publication Data

Names: Spilsbury, Louise.
Title: Combat sports / Louise Spilsbury.
Description: New York : Gareth Stevens Publishing, 2020. | Series: Sports for supergirls
| Includes glossary and index.
Identifiers: ISBN 9781538242179 (pbk.) | ISBN 9781538241905 (library bound)
Subjects: LCSH: Hand-to-hand fighting--Juvenile literature. | Martial arts--Juvenile literature.
| Mixed martial arts--Juvenile literature. | Wrestling--Juvenile literature. | Boxing--Juvenile literature.
| Women athletes--Juvenile literature.
Classification: LCC GV1111.S65 2020 | DDC 796.8--dc23

First Edition

Published in 2020 by
Gareth Stevens Publishing
111 East 14th Street, Suite 349
New York, NY 10003

© 2020 Gareth Stevens Publishing

Produced by Calcium
Editors: Sarah Eason and Jennifer Sanderson
Designers: Clare Webber and Jeni Child

Photo credits: Cover: Shutterstock: ImageFlow; Inside: Shutterstock: 1000 Words: p. 8; Ahturner: pp. 16, 17b;
Bhakpong: p. 29; Dragon Images: p. 5; Everyonephoto Studio: p. 28; Featureflash Photo Agency: p. 37; Iakov
Filimonov: p. 23t; G-Force Vision: p. 32; GP Studio: p. 45; Just dance: pp. 10, 39t; Kzenon: p. 42; Liukov: pp. 30,
31b; Jacob Lund: p. 13b; MikhailSk: p. 31t; Andre Luiz Moreira: p. 41b; A. RICARDO: pp. 3, 7t, 34, 35, 36, 38, 39b,
40, 41t; Romariolen: p. 12; Roselynne: p. 25t; RossHelen: p. 4; S_bukley: p. 6; Joe Seer: p. 7b; Chatchai Somwat:
p. 9; StockphotoVideo: pp. 1, 17t; Testing: p. 25b; Jade ThaiCatwalk: pp. 22, 24, 43; Tumar: p. 18; Undrey:
p. 23b; Wavebreakmedia: p. 11; Zeljkodan: p. 44; Jennifer Simons: p. 33; Wikimedia Commons: Keith Allison:
p. 21; Thatcher Cook for PopTech: p. 14; Miguel Discart: p. 19; Harvey K: p. 15; Mariana Pires23: p. 27; Marcelo
Martins Teixeira: p. 26; U.S. Army: p. 20; U.S. Navy photo by Mass Communication Specialist 2nd Class Elliott
Fabrizio: p. 13t.

CPSIA compliance information: Batch #CS19GS:
For further information contact Gareth Stevens, New York, New York at 1-800-542-2595.

Contents

Chapter 1

Fighting Like a Girl

Combat sports were once seen as male-only territory, but not anymore! Today, women are putting on the gloves and packing a punch with the men in this exciting sporting arena—and they are drawing big crowds, too.

SO, WHAT ARE COMBAT SPORTS?

Combat sports include many different disciplines, from boxing and wrestling to martial arts including tae kwon do, judo, and karate. These may seem like macho sports, but the idea that they are only for men is a thing of the past. Combat sports require mental strength and focus as much as they need a fit, athletic, and strong body. They are great sports for keeping healthy and they can also lead to an exciting sports career.

Combat sports keep participants fit while having fun at the same time.

BODY BENEFITS

Combat sports are the perfect way to work out and feel great. Take a sport like kickboxing, for example. During kickboxing training, participants train full-throttle with their legs and fists, which gives them strong and sleek arms, thighs, and calves. All combat sports build strength and improve stamina and flexibility. Participants leave with a feeling of exhilaration, too.

CHANNELING ENERGY

Combat sports are also a great way to de-stress. After a tough day at school or hours at a desk catching up on homework, hitting the gym is an ideal way to release any tension. While working out, it is easy to forget everyday worries. The buzz athletes get after doing a sport like boxing stays with them for hours afterward. What's not to like?

FACING THE CHALLENGERS

Girls and women who do combat sports battle against more than their opponents. Sports like boxing and jujitsu have been "boys' clubs" for a long time, so many women struggle to get equal funding and coverage by major television networks, and are sometimes excluded from major combat sports events or competitions. This does not stop them. Instead, women in combat sports are achieving success on their own terms by remaining completely determined and dedicated to fighting like a girl.

GIRL TALK

Kickboxing traditionally includes a blend of the punches of boxing and the kicks of karate. When working out, the brain releases chemicals called endorphins. These help boost the athlete's mood.

Combat sports are a great way to cope with stress. Participants can let off steam and de-stress by punching the punching bag and kicking until their legs cannot kick anymore.

Train for the Top!

Combat sports are not for the fainthearted. To do them well, whether they are just trying to keep fit or they want to win competitions, participants need to put their heart and soul into their training. It is important for athletes to come up with a plan and a training schedule and do their best to stick to it. Each athlete is different, so the plan must suit them, their body, and their goals. Athletes may need to adjust their training schedule, for example, if they are injured—training for the top means knowing when to stop.

Case Study

HOLLY HOLM— A MODERN-DAY HEROINE!

Holly Rene Holm was born on October 17, 1981. She is tall, blonde, and glamorous. But more importantly, she is one of the greatest female mixed martial art (MMA) fighters in the world!

Holly competes in the Ultimate Fighting Championship (UFC) and has won several boxing titles. But there is even more to this combat sports superstar—she is the first person to win championships in both boxing and MMA.

FROM GIRLHOOD COMBAT TO QUEEN OF THE RING

So, how did Holly Holm's MMA story start? Holly was born in Albuquerque, New Mexico, and is the youngest of three children. Her father, Roger, is a Church of Christ preacher, and as a fighter, Holly would later be known as "The Preacher's Daughter." In fact, her father has never missed any of Holly's fights, and for years helped her during her boxing matches.

Growing up, Holly played soccer and loved swimming, gymnastics, and diving. Her journey into boxing and kickboxing began with aerobics classes when she was 16 years old. Her cardio-kickboxing instructor, Mike Winkeljohn, saw that Holly could be a great fighter, and began training her. It did not take long for Holly to become a world-class contender, and she has never looked back!

Beating Ronda Rousey (shown here, left) was a big deal for Holly—Ronda is famous for being one of the all-time great female fighters.

GIRL TALK

Holly's most memorable win was in MMA at the 2015 UFCs, when she beat legendary fighter Ronda Rousey to win the bantamweight title. It was the first time Rousey had ever lost an MMA fight!

Holly has hit the big screen too, appearing in the 2016 feature film *Fight Valley*.

Head-to-Head

Traditionally, women have been thought of as not aggressive enough to compete in combat sports. However, many women are ripping up the rule books and showing the world that they will not be trapped by gender stereotypes. These fearless warriors are competing head-to-head in local, national, and international sporting events. In combat sports there can be nail-biting battles, and the results are not always easy to predict. That is because a physically weaker opponent can use technique and training to dominate in a fight against a larger, stronger opponent.

The thrill of being in the ring makes many women want to take up combat sports competitively. They love the "buzz" competing gives them.

STRONGER BODY, STRONGER MIND

When people train in combat sports, they usually discover that, along with building a stronger body, they also improve their focus and concentration, gaining a stronger mind. Combat sport training requires determination, patience, and self-discipline. These attributes can help women have the confidence to handle themselves in any situation.

WOMEN WARRIORS

Women who compete in combat events have to be physically and mentally tough. One sport that works out the entire body and really focuses the mind is Muay Thai , or Thai boxing. Muay Thai is the ancient fighting art of Thailand in which all kinds of hits are allowed. The sport has gained worldwide popularity in recent years. Often referred to as the "art of eight limbs," Thai boxers use their fists, elbows, knees, and shins during kicking, boxing, and grappling moves. Devotees can expect improved stamina, strength, endurance, speed, flexibility, core strength, and self-confidence. Participants should be prepared for a tough workout—it is a very tiring sport because it requires a great deal of strength.

Protective gear is essential for Muay Thai matches to reduce the risk of injuries.

GIRL TALK

For many combat sports, little or no special clothing is required. For most, competitors will just need clothing that is neither too loose nor too restrictive—comfortable clothing that allows freedom of movement—so their usual sports or active gear should be fine, as well as a water bottle and towel. For some combat sports, additional protective gear is needed. For example, Thai boxers wear equipment designed to protect against punches, kicks, and knee and elbow strikes. This includes kickboxing gloves, head guards, and shin guards.

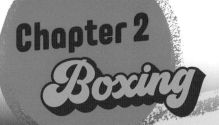

Chapter 2
Boxing

Boxing is one of the most popular contact sports—and women's boxing is an increasingly popular discipline, with greater numbers of enthusiasts joining the sport every year. Although boxers use only their hands, boxing is a complete sport and trains all the muscles in the body.

WHAT IS BOXING?

Boxing is a sport that has been around for thousands of years. There is even evidence of boxing matches in ancient Egypt. Today, a boxing match, or bout, involves two competitors who try to land punches on one another. The aim of the game is to try to knock opponents down and out.

Bouts last 3 to 12 rounds. Each round usually lasts three minutes, and there is a minute-long interval between each round.

BOXING CANNOT BE BEAT!

Boxing is perfect for beginners, and boxing equipment is not too expensive. Participants can box as a workout using a punching bag and never hit another person, or they can box with a sparring partner for fun and exercise. More serious boxers can fight in a fenced-off square, called a ring, with judges scoring points as blows are landed.

A MAN'S WORLD?

In the past, the boxing ring was a man's world, but today there are many female boxers making an impact. Amanda Serrano, AKA "The Real Deal," is a Puerto Rican boxer and mixed martial artist who has held the World Boxing Organization (WBO) female super-bantamweight title since October 2016. Marlen Esparza was the first US woman to qualify for the 2012 Olympics in the first year that women's boxing became an Olympic event.

GIRL TALK

Every official boxing match is run by a referee. If a boxer is knocked down by a punch, the referee or a timekeeper counts off the seconds on their watch. If the boxer does not get up without any help within 20 seconds if they have fallen out of the ring, or 10 seconds if they are within the ring, the referee declares the other boxer the winner.

Referees have the power to signal when a round is over or to stop a match if one fighter cannot take any more punches.

The Gloves Are On!

Those who love the idea of battling it out in a ring can find a coach who will train them and match them to an opponent of a similar weight, age, and level of experience to compete with in boxing bouts. Not everyone has to be a contender—most health clubs and gyms run boxing-style workout classes that combine circuit training with boxing techniques or noncontact boxing classes, where anyone can enjoy boxing for fitness and fun only.

BOXING SMART

Whether fighting for fun or fame, it's worth investing in the right equipment. That includes protective hand bandages under padded gloves and protective headgear to minimize the chances of being injured. In a fight, boxers must also wear a mouth guard. Female boxers are advised to wear breast and crotch protectors. Hair should be tied back or in a bandana, head scarf, or hairnet.

Hand wraps protect a boxer's hands and wrists from being hurt when punching.

WEIGHTY MATTERS

In bouts, competitors fight opponents of the same weight category. There is no universal agreement on weight divisions within women's professional boxing, but amateur weight divisions range from flyweight (106 pounds [48 kg] and under), bantamweight (112 pounds [51 kg] and under), and featherweight (119 pounds [54 kg] and under), right up to heavyweight (179 pounds [81 kg] and under) and super heavyweight (more than 179 pounds [81 kg]). Women's Olympic boxing is restricted to just three weight classes: flyweight, lightweight (123 to 132 pounds [56 to 60 kg]), and middleweight (152 to 165 pounds [69 to 75 kg]).

RULES OF THE GAME

Boxers play by the rules, so competitors must know what is and is not permitted in the ring. Here are some of the rules boxers follow:

- Never hit below the belt.
- Never hold, trip, kick, headbutt, wrestle, bite, spit on, or push an opponent.
- Do not hit with the head, shoulder, forearm, or elbow.
- Never punch an opponent's back or the back of their head or neck.
- Do not hold an opponent and hit them at the same time, or duck so low that the head is below the opponent's belt line.

GIRL TALK

A punching bag is a vital piece of training equipment for a boxer. When using a punching bag in training, boxers put on their gloves and stand facing the punching bag. Then they alternate short punches with longer ones, all the time paying special attention to the power of their hits.

Training as a boxer provides superb allover body conditioning. Benefits include: improved heart and lung function, muscle toning, increased energy, and reduced stress.

Feel the Heat

There are four major organizations that organize world championship boxing bouts: the World Boxing Council (WBC), International Boxing Federation (IBF), World Boxing Association (WBA), and World Boxing Organization (WBO). Women can fight it out against other female boxers in each organization. Female boxers have ratings and rankings just as male boxers do. Within each weight class, women are fighting it out to prove they are the best in their class. Among many famous names, one that stands out is Claressa Shields, AKA "T-Rex."

Case Study

CLARESSA SHIELDS— NATURAL-BORN FIGHTER

Claressa Shields was born on March 17, 1995, in Flint, Michigan. A natural-born fighter, Claressa became the only US fighter, male or female, to win back-to-back Olympic gold medals at the London Games in 2012 and Rio in 2016.

Claressa overcame a challenging childhood to reach stardom. She took up boxing at age 11 after hearing her father Clarence talk about professional boxer Laila Ali. Ali competed from 1999 to 2007 and was the daughter of boxing legend Muhammad Ali. From then on, Claressa trained hard with dedication and determination.

T-REX

Claressa lives up to her nickname—T-Rex. She has a ferocious desire to beat her opponents and a natural ability that shines when you watch her balance and hand speed in action. She is known for her deadly five- and six-punch combinations, but can also fight effectively off the ropes.

FROM AMATEUR TO PROFESSIONAL

Claressa was the best female amateur boxer in the world for years, but after winning two Olympic gold medals, she decided to turn professional and start earning money from her sport in late 2016. She already has professional titles in two weight classes: in the super middleweight and middleweight divisions. Her goal is to win world championships in three weight classes, and there is no doubt that she has the determination to achieve her aim.

GIRL TALK

Claressa is a fan of tennis superstar Serena Williams, and like Serena, Claressa was seen wearing a costume inspired by the movie *Black Panther*, which featured African American superheroes, in 2018. In June, Claressa donned *Black Panther* outfits that gave her the appearance of a modern gladiator and featured her nickname, T-Rex, across the middle.

Claressa (in red) battles against Yenebier Guillén Benitez at the 2015 Pan American Games in Oshawa, Ontario.

Chapter 3
Wrestling

Wrestling is often described as the oldest sport in history—it is the oldest Olympic sport. Steeped in tradition, for thousands of years, wrestling was a hand-to-hand combat sport for men only. But over the past 20 years, the number of female wrestlers has increased dramatically. Now girls and women are competing in this exciting combat sport all over the world.

In a head-to-head sport such as wrestling, you need both skill and strength to win.

WHAT IS WRESTLING?

Wrestling is a simple sport in which two opponents grapple with each other until one manages to throw or force the other to the ground and can be declared the winner. Today there are different styles of wrestling, and wrestling techniques have become quite sophisticated, so it is not always the stronger opponent who comes out on top. Usually, the winner of any wrestling bout has to have the better technique and overall fitness, as well as brute strength.

SPORTING STYLES

The two main wrestling styles are freestyle and Greco-Roman. As its name suggests, freestyle wrestling gives competitors much more freedom. They can use not only their arms and bodies, but also their legs to trip and hold opponents. They can grab an opponent anywhere as they attempt to overpower them. In Greco-Roman wrestling, opponents are not allowed to grab each other below the belt line or use their legs to trip each other or to perform any action.

The ultimate goal in wrestling is to throw and pin the opponent to the ground to achieve a win.

POINTS MEAN PRIZES!

In a wrestling match consisting of three two-minute fights, opponents score points for different takedowns, throws, holds, tilts, and pinning combinations. The scoring system is based on how well a fighter controls their opponent. Sometimes, a winner gains victory by pinning their opponent to the ground. Other times, the winner is the fighter who scores the most points by the end of a match. Points can also be awarded to one opponent if the other opponent does something wrong, such as making an illegal hold.

GIRL TALK

Here are some examples of the points awarded for wrestling moves:

- Takedown (two points): Taking an opponent down to the mat and controlling them
- Escape (one point): Getting away from an opponent when on the mat
- Reversal (two points): Gaining control of an opponent after being held down on the mat

Greco-Roman wrestling matches take place on a round mat made of shock-absorbing rubber.

Smackdown

Wrestling is a great sport for anyone who does not mind getting up close and personal in a one-on-one sport. It is also a great way to get, and stay, fit, because training helps athletes build both strength and a healthy heart and lungs.
An added bonus is that wrestling is also a lot of fun!

LEARNING TO WRESTLE

Anyone interested in learning some wrestling basics can join a local wrestling league or their high school wrestling team. There, they will be able to learn the sport by wrestling with people at the same level and weight as they are. They will also be trained by a qualified coach. Wrestling is physically demanding, so it's good for athletes to spend some time at the gym doing strength workouts, such as regular push-ups, jumping rope, running on a treadmill, or swimming.

Participants need to be incredibly fit to face-off an opponent.

MASTERING THE MOVES

Wrestlers use a combination of attacks, holds, and throws while competing in a match. In a single-leg takedown, a wrestler grabs one of their opponent's legs to throw them off balance and onto the ground. In the duck under, a wrestler ducks under either of the arms of their opponent to gain control of their body. Other moves include the facebuster, in which a wrestler forces their opponent down to the mat face-first.

TOP TIP!

In wrestling, the aim of the game is to pin an opponent to the ground. The best way to stay standing is to keep a low center of gravity. To do this, wrestlers take up a crouched position. They keep their legs wide and their torso low to the ground with their weight spread evenly between both feet, while they balance on the balls of their feet.

GIRL TALK

To minimize the chances of being injured in the ring, wrestlers wear various pieces of protective gear. This includes a mouth guard, a singlet (a one-piece article of clothing which covers the body down to the mid-thigh), wrestling shoes, and protective headgear. Female wrestlers usually wear an athletic support or a sports bra for protection, too.

Famous wrestler Asuka is known for her colorful hair and stylish kicks and submission holds.

Reach for the Stars

Many participants wrestle for fun and for fitness, but others choose to compete in tournaments and some even become wrestling stars. Wrestling at any level instills great qualities, including self-discipline, self-control, and confidence. Athletes also master perseverance and the willingness to work hard, while understanding that they must make sacrifices to be the best in their sport. For some, wrestling also brings fame, medals, trophies, and financial rewards.

GIRL TALK

In wrestling tournaments, fighters compete against opponents in the same weight category. There are 10 different weight classes in total, ranging from 110 pounds to 161 pounds (50 kg to 73 kg) in freestyle wrestling and from 121 pounds to 287 pounds (55 kg to 130 kg) in Greco-Roman. Olympic gold-medal winner Helen Maroulis competes in the women's 117-pound (53 kg) and 121-pound (55 kg) categories.

Helen Maroulis takes down fellow American Whitney Conder in the finals of the 2016 US Olympic wrestling team trials.

HELEN MAROULIS— GOING FOR GOLD!

At the 2016 Olympics in Rio de Janeiro, Brazil, Helen Maroulis became the first-ever American to win an Olympic gold medal in women's freestyle wrestling. She wrestled four matches in the preliminaries, before stepping into the arena in front of expectant crowds to defeat Japan's Saori Yoshida in the finals.

STEPS TO STARDOM

Helen was born in Rockville, Maryland, on September 19, 1991, to John and Paula Maroulis, whose parents had emigrated to the United States from the Greek island Kálamos in the 1960s. Helen began wrestling by chance when she was seven years old, after her mother asked her to stand in as a partner for her younger brother, who had just taken up the sport. After two weeks of training, she was hooked on the sport and became determined to be a great wrestler herself.

Helen wrestled throughout high school, often against boys, and then competed on the women's wrestling team in St. Louis, Missouri, while attending the Missouri Baptist University, before transferring to compete for Simon Fraser University in Burnaby, British Columbia, Canada. To achieve her Olympic dream, she later dedicated her time to training at the U.S. Olympic Education Center at Northern Michigan University.

As well as taking part in wrestling competitions, Helen travels the world to promote the sport. She also runs clinics for wrestlers of all ages in order to share her love for the sport.

To secure her Olympic gold medal, Helen had to take down Saori Yoshida, winner of the previous three gold medals in the event!

Chapter 4
Tae Kwon Do

The sport of tae kwon do goes back more than 2,000 years to various ancient Korean forms of martial arts. The modern form of tae kwon do practiced today was established in 1955. It is most famous for the awesome hopping, jumping, and flying kicks that impress audiences everywhere.

THE FOOT AND THE FIST

The name "tae kwon do" translates to "the way of the foot and the fist." "Tae" means to break or attack with the foot, "kwon" means to break with the fist, and "do" translates to "the art or way." Tae kwon do was introduced to the United States during the 1950s when a group of Korean master instructors traveled there to showcase their skills. Since then, tae kwon do has grown in popularity and has become an international sport.

Participants can be injured during tae kwon do, so they wear protective equipment including a helmet, a protective vest, arm guards, shin guards, and a crotch or groin guard.

Training in tae kwon do techniques is good for the body and the mind.

Training in tae kwon do techniques is good for the body and the mind.

TAE KWON DO FOR LIFE

Tae kwon do is very dynamic and uses a lot of high standing and jump kicks as well as punches. However, tae kwon do teaches more than kicking and punching skills. It is a discipline that teaches self-defense and spiritual development through training the body and mind. The idea is that when people do tae kwon do, they should make their mind peaceful and synchronize their thoughts with their movements, so that their mind and body work together in harmony. Learning tae kwon do helps people develop as individuals and greatly improves their general health, strength, flexibility, control, and self-confidence in everyday life.

GIRL TALK

There are many different tactics that can be used in tae kwon do, including:

• Roundhouse: This is a flying kick, in which the attacker has both feet off the ground.

• Ax kick: This is a move in which the attacker, standing on one leg, drops their other heel onto the opponent's head.

• Skip kick: In this kick, the kicking leg is swapped in midair.

• Spin kicks: These involve rotating the entire body and head before the kick is released.

• Tiger claw: This strike is made using the space between the index finger and thumb.

Performing moves like the ax kick takes a lot of practice.

Strike and Defend

Doing tae kwon do means learning to attack and defend using different parts of the body. "Tae" refers to the feet, legs, and lower torso. Trainees learn to use their lower torso to provide the force needed to do hopping, jumping, and flying kicks. To strike, they use their upper body, elbows, and arms as well as the hands, fingertips, wrists, and fists. There are a variety of different moves to learn, requiring patience, self-discipline, dedicated training, and seriously flexible legs.

TEACHING TAE KWON DO

Tae kwon do trainers teach individual techniques of kicking, punching, and blocking (used to stop and deflect an incoming attack), which are practiced in combined series of techniques in traditional sets known as hyung. Students also practice basic sparring combinations, which are short, set sequences of attack and defense on which pairs of trainees work together. Only when trainees have mastered these basic skills should they start sparring with opponents. And even in sparring, trainees usually stop blows just before the point of hitting an opponent.

Trainees learn to perfect the basic skills of tae kwon do before beginning to fight competitively.

TAE KWON DO BELTS AND RANKS

A dobok is the traditional uniform, or suit, people wear when doing tae kwon do. Like many martial arts, tae kwon do has ranks, called Kup. As they progress with their training, athletes wear different grade belts over their dobok to tell others what rank they have achieved. New students begin at the tenth Kup, which is a white belt, and advance through different colored belts to the first Kup, which is a red belt with a black stripe. Students then advance into an intermediate rank called black-belt candidate. After this, students take a dan test. If successful, they become a first-dan black belt.

It takes a minimum of four years' training to earn a black belt.

GIRL TALK

Blocking is a vital tool in any athlete's tae kwon do skill set. It is a way of stopping strikes and can involve different parts of the arm and hand held in different positions. Different blocks are used for particular kinds of attacks. They can also be combined with another punch or kick to make a counterattack. For example, in the knife-hand block, the hand is kept in a knife-hand position to block attacks to the torso. A palm block is an open hand raised up to shoulder height and thrust directly down to stop the attacker.

Learning to block different kinds of attacks is vital in order to stay the course in a tae kwon do match.

Fighting for Fame

Today, tae kwon do has become a global sport and gained an international reputation. It became an Olympic sport at the 2000 Games in Sydney, Australia. In a tae kwon do tournament or championship, competitors face each other on a mat inside a 26 x 26 foot (8 x 8 m) zone. They fight each other over three rounds, with each round lasting two minutes. There are usually four judges, one standing at each corner of the combat area, and a referee who can stand within the combat area.

GIRL TALK

The aim of tae kwon do is to land accurate kicks and punches on the scoring areas (head or torso) of an opponent. For example, a kick or punch to an opponent's torso scores one point. An extra point is awarded if the athlete's back was toward their opponent at the point of contact. Hence, spinning kicks score two points. If the scores are level after three rounds, a fourth, sudden-death round is held to determine the winner. Today, in important tournaments, scoring is often carried out by an electronic impact scoring system.

Tae kwon do athlete Kimia Alizadeh Zonoozi (kneeling) celebrates becoming the first Iranian woman to win a medal at the Olympic Games, in 2016.

JACKIE GALLOWAY—TAE KWON DO TALENT

When an athlete wins an Olympic medal, they are usually applauded by just one country. But when US athlete Jackie Galloway, whose mother is Mexican and her father American, won an Olympic bronze medal at Rio in 2016, she had supporters cheering her on loudly from both sides of the border.

A FAMILY AFFAIR

Jaqueline Rose Sanchez Galloway was born on December 27, 1995, and raised in Texas. She began practicing tae kwon do at a dojo (martial arts training hall) run by her parents when she was seven years old. Jackie was determined to make it to the top from an early age, and her parents gave her the skills and support she needed to progress. Her family is still involved in her training. Her father is her coach, and her brother is her training partner.

Because her heritage gave Galloway dual citizenship, at 14 she took the chance to join Mexico's national team and moved to Mexico City. It was hard being alone, but, she says, it helped her develop into the competitor she is today. In 2012, she was an alternate for the London Olympics. After that, she returned to Texas and joined Team USA to train for the Rio Games in 2016, where she brought home the bronze medal.

Tae kwon do is one of the most popular Olympic sports. Spectators fill the arena, waiting for the competition to begin.

Chapter 5
Brazilian Jujitsu

Brazilian jujitsu is a combat sport with origins in judo and Japanese jujitsu. Unlike the Japanese combat sports from which it was born, Brazilian jujitsu takes place completely on the floor, so competitors learn how to defend themselves even when they are lying on the ground.

THE GENTLE ART

Anyone who has fought and been beaten by a Brazilian jujitsu expert would say there is nothing gentle about the experience. So, why is this combat sport known as the gentle art? It is gentle because you do not have to be the bigger or stronger opponent to win a fight. A smaller, weaker person who is calm, focused, flexible, and concentrates their efforts on skillfully controlling their opponent, can win. That is why women, men, and children as young as four years old are flocking to clubs to learn Brazilian jujitsu.

When athletes are pinned down painfully by an opponent, it is hard to believe that jujitsu is known as the gentle art!

A GAME OF HUMAN CHESS

Brazilian jujitsu is also described as a game of human chess. That is because during a match, opponents are constantly adapting their strategy to one another's movements, just as one would in a game of chess. An opponent has to use different tactics and techniques in order to defeat the other. They have to spot an opponent's weaknesses, using their strengths against them and working out how to avoid an opponent's strengths. As people become more skilled at Brazilian jujitsu, they learn more techniques and strategies to counter their opponent's moves in the game.

GOOD FOR YOU!

Brazilian jujitsu is a great way to get fit and keep in shape. It is a unique workout that includes floor-based exercises, which combine yoga, pilates, and CrossFit training to help participants become fit and strong. Regular training on the mat and the patience required to learn and master new techniques also give people the confidence, perseverance, and determination to tackle any job, problem, or goal they meet in life.

GIRL TALK

Some girls and women choose to do combat sports such as Brazilian jujitsu for self-defense. Brazilian jujitsu gives participants the knowledge and skills to outsmart someone bigger than them. It can also help them survive an attack whether they are on their feet or find themselves on the ground.

CrossFit training gives athletes a whole-body workout and helps build strength. Workouts vary a lot so athletes are very seldom bored.

No Pain, No Gain

Learning any new skill takes time and effort, but if people are prepared to give some sweat and work hard, they will get so much out of Brazilian jujitsu. The best way to learn is in classes at a training school. There, an experienced instructor can demonstrate the correct way to grapple and fight opponents on the ground. Classes always start with a warm-up, then participants will begin to learn some moves and take some falls.

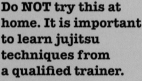

Do NOT try this at home. It is important to learn jujitsu techniques from a qualified trainer.

NEW MOVES

One basic technique participants will learn is the forward roll. This is a way of falling safely that helps people avoid injury. They start with a neutral stance: standing with feet shoulder-width apart, shoulders back, and spine straight. Then they step forward with one foot, reach for their opposite leg, and roll from one shoulder to the opposite hip. Some simple attacks include the front snap punch, in which athletes put their left foot forward, keep up their fists to protect their face, jab their left fist at the opponent, and then strike them with the right fist.

CHOKES AND LOCKS

To beat or defend themselves against an opponent, athletes also need chokes and locks. In the cross choke, for example, they put their arms in front of their opponent's chest, holding onto their collars in a crossing frame until they submit. Locks also stop opponents in their tracks. For example, using a double-wrist control to trap an opponent's arm (bent in an "L" shape) leaves the opponent unable to move their elbow and shoulder joints.

GETTING THE GEAR

A gi is the robe worn during classes and competitions. It should fit well and be comfortable. The sleeves and trousers should not be too long and the gi must be loose enough that it does not restrict movement. Participants will also need some protective gear. Some wear knee braces, ear guards, a mouth guard, and a crotch protector to reduce the risk of injury. They can also protect their fingers and toes with athletic tape, because most places do not allow shoes on the mats.

GIRL TALK

To hold the gi robe in place, jujitsu athletes wear a belt. Beginners start with a white belt and, as they gain new skills, they progress through different-colored belts until they reach the highest level, which is the black belt.

The easiest way to tie the belt is to loop it around the waist, then slip the left side underneath and out through the top. The ends are then tied in a knot and pulled tight.

In It to Win It

Whether athletes are competing in a Brazilian jujitsu tournament or sparring with a training partner, they should go all out to win. They should make full use of grappling techniques to force the fight to the ground and then apply lock and choke holds to get their opponent into a position from which they cannot escape. When an opponent taps three times, it means they submit and admit defeat.

GIRL TALK

Superstars like Cindy Omatsu know that learning chokes and locks is not enough. Success depends on having all the techniques available to you but also a deeper understanding of why certain techniques work and knowing when to use them. Even the best practitioners of Brazilian jujitsu can be beaten by an opponent who uses distance, timing, and positioning to spoil the other fighter's chances of using the strongest parts of their game.

Brazilian jujitsu teaches brain over brawn. A smart fighter can take down the strongest opponent.

CINDY OMATSU—BELLE OF THE BLACK BELTS

In 2002, Cindy Omatsu made history when she became the first Asian-American and the first woman outside of Brazil to be promoted to black-belt level in Brazilian jujitsu. Cindy felt a great connection with jujitsu from the time she started learning, and is one of the most famous female blackbelts in the sport.

STARTING OUT

Cynthia Ann "Cindy" Omatsu was born on January 19, 1961, and raised in Torrance, California. Her grandparents came to the United States from Japan. Cindy loved sports in her youth, but started training in Brazilian jujitsu only in 1994 to learn some self-defense after there had been a series of attacks on young women in her neighborhood.

Every athlete trains hard. Here, Cindy Omatsu (left) trains with Leka Vieira, her coach and mentor.

Cindy devoted as many hours to training as she could, spending most time on the mat fighting men because there were so few women in the sport during the early days. This focused her mind and helped her develop ways to compete against larger opponents. In 2001, World Champion female instructor Leka Vieira moved to the United States from Brazil, and Omatsu immediately joined her women-only class, becoming one of the star pupils. Just a year later, she had gained her black belt.

Chapter 6
Mixed Martial Arts

Mixed martial arts (MMA) is one of the fastest-growing professional sports in the world. As its name suggests, this high-octane combat style is a mix of martial arts that involves different types of fighting technique. In this full-contact sport, opponents use their hands and legs in bouts that involve punching, kicking, and grappling, both standing and on the floor. Be warned: MMA is not for the fainthearted!

IN THE MIX

MMA combines elements of various martial arts and Olympic sports such as boxing, kickboxing, karate, jujitsu, Muay Thai, judo, tae kwon do, and wrestling. An MMA contest typically consists of a total of three rounds, each of which lasts five minutes. Championship fights are different. In these big competitions, a contest lasts five grueling rounds.

The fearsome and famous Brazilian MMA fighter Amanda Nunes takes down another victim.

WOMEN IN MMA

Women had been fighting MMA for a while, but it was only in 2011 that Ultimate Fighting Championship (UFC) president Dana White famously said that women would never fight in the UFC. Well-known female fighter Ronda "Rowdy" Rousey persuaded him otherwise, and in November 2012, the fight promotion announced she was signed on their books. Soon, women like Rousey were headlining main events, filling arena seats, and proving that their fights are every bit as exciting to watch and be part of as men's.

GIRL TALK

The UFC is the premier MMA organization and it has been the driving force that has helped make MMA so popular. The UFC has done such a great job of marketing its brand that many people think UFC is the same as MMA.

WEIGHT CLASSES

There are fewer weight divisions in women's MMA than men's, and some MMA organizations that recognize women's championships usually have titles at the lower end of the table only—for example, strawweight, flyweight, bantamweight, and featherweight. Weight classes are:

Strawweight: 106-115 pounds (48-52 kg)
Flyweight: To 125 pounds (57 kg)
Bantamweight: To 135 pounds (61 kg)
Featherweight: To 145 pounds (66 kg)
Lightweight: To 155 pounds (70 kg)
Super lightweight: To 165 pounds (75 kg)
Welterweight: To 170 pounds (77 kg)
Middleweight: To 185 pounds (84 kg)
Super middleweight: To 195 pounds (89 kg)
Light heavyweight: To 205 pounds (93 kg)
Cruiserweight: To 225 pounds (102 kg)
Heavyweight: To 265 pounds (120 kg)

Ronda Rousey (right) was a trailblazer for women's MMA while she fought the sport.

Cage Fighting

Often MMA is referred to as cage fighting. That is because UFC contests take place in a fighting area that is usually octagonal in shape and surrounded by a metal or net cage. The cage means a fighter can use different kinds of strategies and it prevents a fighter from falling out onto the floor or onto spectators.

GIRL TALK

A fighter can pin an opponent in the area where the fence meets the mat, and then strike them repeatedly with punches. It also allows for defensive moves, such as using the cage as support to fight off takedown attempts or to escape from beneath an opponent.

TALKING TACTICS

In an MMA cage, two competitors attack each other using a variety of martial arts techniques, including punches, kicks, locks, chokes, takedowns, and throws. They can use wrestling, judo, and other clinching and grappling techniques to get into a good position for controlling their opponent and to get them on the ground. They can use combinations of boxing, kickboxing, and Muay Thai techniques, among others, to strike and attack their opponent.

An MMA contest includes stand-up fighting, clinch fighting, and ground fighting.

ROSE NAMAJUNAS— MMA THUG

Rose Namajunas grew up in a rough neighborhood where she witnessed violence. From a young age, she acted tough to protect herself. This tough act earned her the nickname "Thug Rose," which stayed with her when she became an MMA champion.

ROSE ON THE RISE

Born June 29, 1992, Rose grew up in Milwaukee, Wisconsin, the second child of Lithuanian immigrants. She took up tae kwon do when she was five years old and earned her junior black belt at nine. She also learned judo and karate, and did wrestling in high school. In fact, Rose has tried almost every martial art there is! At 17, she joined an MMA academy and fell in love with the sport.

From that point on, Rose never looked back. Today, she competes in the UFC women's strawweight division. In spite of her nickname, Namajunas rarely trash-talks her opponents before a fight. "Thug Rose" makes an appearance only during a contest when she needs to be super tough. When fights are over, a gentler Rose enjoys spending her time gardening and plans to become a farmer in the future, the other ambition she has held since she was a little girl!

Rose Namajunas learned multiple martial arts from a young age. It takes years of dedication and hard training to be successful at MMA.

In an MMA contest there are several ways a competitor can win. A knockout is when a powerful punch or blow either knocks an opponent out or renders them unable to continue fighting. A submission is when one fighter is in trouble and admits defeat by tapping the mat or their opponent with their hand. If the fight goes the distance, and lasts all three or five rounds, judges decide the winner based on the scores awarded throughout the fight.

MMA fighters score two points for a clean kick during a match.

SCORING A FIGHT

Judges decide who wins fights according to a variety of criteria. In a contest, there are three judges sitting outside the cage, each one watching the fight from a different angle. They adjudicate a contestant's techniques, such as their striking, grappling, and defense skills, as well as their ability to control the fighting area. They use a 10-point system, in which the winner of a round scores 10 points and the loser gets 9 or fewer. A match can be stopped by the referee, the fight doctor, or the judge. A referee stoppage occurs when the referee determines that an opponent is unable to defend themselves properly in the face of an attack.

GIRL TALK

Here are two winning moves MMA fighters use:

- Rear naked choke: A contestant who is lying down wraps one arm around their opponent's neck, reinforcing that grip with the other arm to force a tapout.

- Takedown: A contestant either shoots in or from a clinch position (when fighters have grabbed hold of each other), forces an opponent onto the ground, and gets on top of them.

If an athlete can get on top of an opponent and pin them on the ground, victory is theirs!

NO RULES

Some people think that MMA has no rules. In fact, it has many. The rules include the size of the fighting area, specifications about the way hands are wrapped under gloves, and standards about judging and fouls, among other things. There are more than 25 official fouls, including no head butting, no bending of fingers, and no behavior that risks injuring an opponent. Most fouls are punished by a point being deducted from a score, but if a referee spots a bad and intentional foul, a competitor can be disqualified.

Referees keep a close eye on all attacks and injuries in an MMA match.

Fighting Like a Lioness

While MMA is mainly dominated by men, the sport does have a quickly growing number of fearsome female athletes. In the United States, things really took off for women's combat sport after the *Ultimate Fighter* reality television series and MMA competition, which made household names of female fighters such as Ronda Rousey. Today, there are numerous MMA female stars who are fighting like lionesses.

GIRL TALK

In professional MMA competitions, female fighters wear gloves, chest protectors, and shorts (similar to the shorts worn in boxing and Muay Thai). This type of clothing is often referred to as fightwear. In amateur fights or training sessions, people also wear head guards, kneepads, and shin protection.

MMA gloves make sure that fighters' hands stay protected.

AMANDA NUNES— A LIONESS ROARS!

Amanda Nunes's nickname in the world of combat sports is "Lioness of the Ring," and like her namesake in the animal kingdom, Amanda is one of the most dangerous predators on the MMA scene. She currently fights for the UFC, where she is the reigning women's bantamweight champion.

BORN IN BRAZIL

Amanda Nunes was born May 30, 1988, and grew up in a small town outside of Salvador, Bahia, Brazil. Her mother had been a boxer and Amanda learned boxing, karate, and capoeira (a traditional fight–dance) from a young age. She loved soccer, too. She was 16 when she became hooked on Brazilian jujitsu. She moved to Salvador, where she lived, worked, and trained at an all-male gym, thinking about fights 24 hours a day. It was a tough life, but it also helped turn her into the lioness that she is today.

Later, Amanda moved to the United States, first living in New Jersey, where she trained at AMA Fight Club, and then in Miami, where she trained at MMA Masters. Amanda made her first public appearance at an MMA tournament in March 8, 2008. She lost, but this strengthened her resolve and determination. Since then, she has won most of the bouts she has ever fought.

Amanda Nunes celebrates winning the Bantamweight Ultimate Fighting Championship in Brazil in 2018.

Fighter Amanda Nunes weighs in and shows off her muscles to her opponents before a fight.

Becoming a Supergirl

No matter how much fighting talk there is between opponents before and even during a match, or during weigh-ins and face-offs, after a bout ends, combat fighters shake hands, embrace, bow, or congratulate each other. While individuals compete to become the best they can be, the girls and women in combat sports respect and support each other and encourage each other to succeed. After reading so many positives about combat sports, perhaps you would like to try them out for yourself?

GIRL POWER

Becoming a supergirl does not necessarily mean becoming a superstar. Learning combat sports will give you confidence, strength, fitness, and a determination to succeed in all walks of life. Those are the characteristics that make a true supergirl. Many supergirls will simply enjoy doing combat sports as a hobby or a regular workout and appreciate the opportunity to meet other like-minded girls and women—combat clubs are a great place to make friends and to have fun.

The girls you spar with might become great friends outside the gym.

BEING A CONTENDER

If you do want to compete in tournaments, perhaps even at an international level, you need to be prepared to work for it. To become a successful fighter in combat sports, as is the case with other kinds of sport, most people start training and competing at a young age. If your aim is to compete at a high level, you will have to put in hours, weeks, and indeed months of practice. It will not be easy, but if you really have the dedication and determination to succeed, why not give it a go?

CAREERS IN COMBAT!

As well as doing combat sports for fun and to compete at a high level, some people find a different kind of career in the combat sporting world. Some combat supergirls become coaches and mentors. Others get jobs organizing events, which might involve scoping out and hiring venues. Some people work in jobs promoting combat competitions to ensure plenty of people come to watch them. Or you could even be a sports journalist, writing reports about combat sport events and stars.

GIRL TALK

If you become a martial arts instructor in the future, you will help to train the next generation of martial arts stars by demonstrating techniques, watching over sparring sessions, and helping students to develop both the physical and mental strength they will need to succeed.

Becoming a martial arts instructor is a rewarding career—you would help young athletes achieve their dreams and pass on your hard-won skills.

Try It Out!

Now that you have found out just how great girls can be at combat sports, it's time to find your own inner supergirl and try them out for yourself! The term "combat sports" covers such a large number of different sports, there is sure to be one discipline that appeals to you.

Regardless of what you are into, whether it is boxing, judo, Muay Thai , karate, tae kwon do, or MMA, there are plenty of clubs around the United States that you can join to learn about combat sports.

MUAY THAI

If Muay Thai is your thing, you can take lessons at the Muay Thai School USA, in Hollywood, California. For more information, go to: www.muaythaischoolusa.com

The United States Muay Thai Federation (USMF) website has links to gyms where you can learn and train in Muay Thai. Log on at: www.unitedstatesmuaythaifederation.org/pages/usmf-member-gyms

BOXING

If you want to find a US Boxing registered club in your area, go to: www.teamusa.org/usa-boxing/membership/find-a-club

No excuses! You should easily be able to find a training gym in or near your hometown.

WRESTLING

Women's wrestling is a growing combat sport, so finding a club near you should not be too difficult. To find wrestling clubs in your state, check out: www.teamusa.org/usa-wrestling/clubs

TAE KWON DO

Read all about how to find the best tae kwon do club for you at: www.teamusa.org/usa-taekwondo/v2-getting-started-in-taekwondo/how-to-find-a-taekwondo-school. You could also log on at: https://ataonline.com/taekwondo

BRAZILIAN JUJITSU

If you want to learn Brazilian jujitsu, find a club or trainer near you at: www.usjjf.org/school-directory.html

MIXED MARTIAL ARTS

There is a list of certified training centers for MMA at: https://ummaf.org/trainers/training-centers

Combat sports are a great way to keep fit, strong, and mentally tough. Simple skills like skipping and running are often part of the training.

GIRL TALK

Once you know what sort of class you want to join, speak to a few different teachers, read some reviews, and maybe even ask if you can sit in and watch a class before you sign up. This is the best way to find out what happens in the lessons and whether the class is right for you. Even if a class looks challenging, it is worth giving it a chance—you are there to learn a new skill, be healthy, and have fun!

Glossary

center of gravity the point in an object where its weight is balanced

circuit training a fast-paced exercise program in which participants do one exercise for 30 seconds to 5 minutes, and then move on to a different exercise

contact sports sports in which the participants necessarily come into bodily contact with one another

core strength the strength of the muscles within the torso

CrossFit a high-intensity fitness program that combines elements from several sports and types of exercise

disciplines different fields or branches of something, such as sport

exhilaration a feeling of excitement and happiness

fouls actions that break the rules of a sport or game, especially those involving interference with an opponent

gender the state of being male or female

illegal against laws or rules

journalist a person who writes for newspapers, magazines, or news websites, or prepares news to be broadcast

martial arts various sports, which originated chiefly in Japan, Korea, and China, as forms of self-defense or attack

pilates a form of exercise that is typically done on a floor mat and aims to strengthen the muscles, especially in the torso

punching bag a stuffed or inflated bag that hangs down and can be punched for exercise or for boxing training

referee an official who watches a game or match closely to make sure that the players or contestants obey the rules

round a division of a contest such as a boxing or wrestling match

sparring training in a combat sport without landing heavy blows on an opponent

spiritual relating to the human spirit, the way people feel about life and what it means

stamina physical or mental strength that allows people to continue doing something for a long time

stereotypes widely held but fixed and oversimplified images or ideas of particular types of people or things

torso the trunk or central part of the body that does not include the head, arms, or legs

treadmill a device consisting of a continuous moving belt on which to walk or run

yoga a type of exercise in which you move your body into various positions in order to become more fit or flexible, to improve your breathing, and to relax your mind

For More Information

BOOKS

Doeden, Matt. *Combat Sports* (Summer Olympic Sports). Mankato, MN: Amicus Ink, 2016.

Graubart, Norman D. *Laila Ali: Champion Boxer* (Exceptional African Americans). New York, NY: Enslow Publishing, 2015.

Johnson, Nathan. *Kickboxing and MMA* (Mastering Martial Arts). Broomall, PA: Mason Crest, 2015.

Proudfit, Benjamin. *Charlotte Flair* (Superstars of Wrestling). New York, NY: Gareth Stevens Publishing, 2018.

Wood, Alix. *Tae Kwon Do* (A Kid's Guide to Martial Arts). New York, NY: PowerKids Press, 2013.

WEBSITES

Discover more about careers in combat sports at:
www.allaboutcareers.com/careers/career-path/combat-sports-boxing-judo-muay-thai-others

Read about the origins and history of MMA at:
https://kids.britannica.com/students/article/mixed-martial-arts-MMA/626791/334015-toc

You can learn more about Brazilian jujitsu at the US Brazilian Ju-jitsu Federation website:
www.usjjf.org

Learn more about combat sports at:
www.wikihow.com/Category:Combat-Sports

Publisher's note to educators and parents:

Our editors have carefully reviewed these websites to ensure that they are suitable for students. Many websites change frequently, however, and we cannot guarantee that a site's future contents will continue to meet our high standards of quality and educational value. Be advised that students should be closely supervised whenever they access the Internet.